GW01406749

Original title:
Joy Boost

Author: Clement Portlander
ISBN HARDBACK: 978-9916-88-246-7
ISBN PAPERBACK: 978-9916-88-247-4

Radiant Bridges of Connection

Across the river, a bridge so bright,
Connecting hearts in the soft moonlight.
With every step, a story unfolds,
A tapestry woven, in warmth it holds.

Two souls meet where the waters flow,
Together they learn, together they grow.
Each laugh a step, each tear a thread,
Binding their paths, where love is spread.

Poems of the Heart's Happiness

In the garden where laughter blooms,
Every petal dances, dispelling glooms.
Sunshine creeps through leaves above,
Whispering tales of everlasting love.

With every heartbeat, a verse is penned,
In rhythm and rhyme, where sorrows end.
Joyful echoes in the gentle breeze,
Paint the world with moments that please.

Songs Carried by the Breeze

Gentle whispers float through the air,
Melodies drifting without a care.
Each note a story, each sigh a dream,
Riding the wind, like sunlight's beam.

From mountain tops to valleys wide,
The songs travel far, with the tide.
Voices unite, in harmony found,
With every heartbeat, a joyful sound.

Streams of Serendipity

In the quiet moments when paths collide,
Magic appears, like the ocean's tide.
Fortunes unfold, like petals at dawn,
In the dance of fate, we're never alone.

Winding rivers of chance and grace,
Lead us to wonders, in love's embrace.
Unexpected joys, like stars in the night,
Illuminate our souls, with pure delight.

A Tidal Wave of Smiles

In the morning light, hopes arise,
Children's laughter, a sweet surprise.
Joy cascades like waves on sand,
Embracing hearts across the land.

With every glance, a spark ignites,
A flicker of warmth in long, cold nights.
Together we dance, let worries cease,
Caught in the tide of purest peace.

Ripples spread from each bright beam,
A world united, the power of a dream.
In the ocean of joy, we find our way,
Riding the current, come what may.

Refrains of a Wearied Soul

In the stillness of night, I trace
The shadows lingering, a quiet place.
Whispers of dreams begin to fade,
Echoes of hopes in the twilight shade.

Each step I take wears heavy shoes,
The weight of the world, I cannot choose.
Yet in the silence, a flicker calls,
A melody sweet that softly enthralls.

Through weary paths, a song will rise,
A gentle hymn to the starry skies.
For even in darkness, the heart can hear,
The softest of notes, a reason to cheer.

Fables of a Beaming Heart

In the garden of dreams, petals unfurl,
Stories of joy in the morning swirl.
A beaming heart, like sunshine bright,
Spreads warmth and love, taking flight.

With every tale, new worlds are spun,
Adventures await for everyone.
Lessons of kindness, woven in time,
Chants of hope in a rhythmic rhyme.

In laughter's embrace, we twirl and sway,
Creating fables that light our way.
Together we weave the fabric of bliss,
A tapestry rich in shared happiness.

The Taste of Laughter's Embrace

In the air, joy's light dance,
Echoes of glee, a sweet trance.
Hearts entwined in mirth's bright glow,
Moments shared, letting time flow.

Whispers of laughter, soft and warm,
Gathering souls, a vibrant swarm.
Fingers touch, smiles brightly grow,
In laughter's embrace, love will show.

Vibrations of Vibrant Spirits

Colors blend in joyful song,
Where lively hearts forever throng.
Rhythms call, the night divine,
In every beat, our souls align.

Energy flows like a wild breeze,
In every laugh, we seek to please.
With every twirl, we paint the air,
Vibrations echo everywhere.

Luminary of Sweet Sojourns

A journey bright with every glance,
In twilight's glow, we take a chance.
With hearts aglow, we roam and play,
Each step a note, in bright ballet.

Guided by dreams, we wander wide,
In the night, our hopes abide.
Under stars that brightly gleam,
Together we weave our shared dream.

Revelations in Beaming Souls

In quiet moments, truth unveils,
A tapestry of love prevails.
Eyes meet in an eternal sync,
Hearts speak softly, more than we think.

Through silences, connections bloom,
In shared breaths, dispel the gloom.
Revelations sparkle bright and bold,
In every heartbeat, stories told.

The Playful Wind's Advice

Whispering secrets through the trees,
A tug at your heart, a gentle tease.
Dance with the leaves, let worries drift,
In the playful wind, find your gift.

Chase the clouds, let your spirit soar,
What once felt heavy is light evermore.
Trust the breeze to guide your way,
Embrace the joy of a brand new day.

Stitches of Serenity

In quiet corners, shadows play,
Threads of peace weave night and day.
With every stitch, a story spun,
In the fabric of life, we are one.

Gather the moments, soft and dear,
Wrap them close, keep them near.
In gentle seams, find your place,
A quilt of calm, a warm embrace.

The Canvas of Cheerfulness

Bright colors splash across the sky,
Brush strokes of laughter, oh so spry.
Each hue a note in a joyful song,
On this canvas of cheer, we all belong.

Let your heart be the artist's hand,
Create a masterpiece, colorful and grand.
With every stroke, let happiness flow,
In the art of living, let your spirit glow.

Unfolding Stories of Laughter

Pages turning in the breeze,
Tales of giggles, moments of ease.
Every chuckle a line well-spun,
In the book of life, laughter is fun.

Gather around, share your tale,
With joy and wit, let laughter sail.
In every story, sunshine peeks,
Unfolding happiness, heartily speaks.

Embracing the Moment

In the silence, whispers call,
Time stands still, we feel it all.
Holding hands, with hearts aglow,
Every breath, a river's flow.

Under stars, we share our dreams,
Life is richer than it seems.
In this space, we find our way,
Together here, come what may.

Sweet Songs of Liveliness

The morning sings, a fresh refrain,
Nature's pulse, our hearts sustain.
Sunlight dances on the leaves,
In pure joy, we believe.

Laughter echoes, children play,
Chasing shadows, come what may.
Every moment filled with cheer,
Life's sweet song is crystal clear.

Unrestrained Bliss

In wild fields, we run and leap,
Chasing dreams, no need for sleep.
With every laugh, we touch the sky,
In this magic, we can fly.

Free as birds in endless flight,
Hearts entwined, we shine so bright.
Every heartbeat, a joyful tune,
In this bliss, we've found our boon.

Curves of Contentment

The sunset paints the world in gold,
Soft embraces, love unfolds.
In cozy nooks, we find our peace,
In gentle moments, worries cease.

Time flows slowly, sweet and kind,
In simple joys, our hearts aligned.
With every glance, a silent vow,
In curves of contentment, here and now.

Chasing the Light

In the dawn's delicate glow,
We run where the wild winds blow.
Fingers brush the morning dew,
Illuminated dreams come true.

Through golden fields we race,
With laughter, we find our place.
Each ray a guide on the way,
Chasing the light, come what may.

Serenade of Smiles

A melody bright in the air,
Echoes of joy everywhere.
In the corners of our hearts,
A symphony of sweet parts.

With every glance, a new tune,
Dancing beneath the warm moon.
Together we create this song,
Where smiles tell us we belong.

The Magic of Merriment

In the laughter, we find our spark,
Filling shadows, lighting the dark.
Every giggle, a piece of art,
A treasure that glows in the heart.

With every cheer and playful jest,
We weave a tapestry blessed.
In moments rich with delight,
We unleash the magic of light.

Painting the Sky with Cheer

Brushes dipped in hues so bright,
We color the canvas of the night.
With each stroke, our spirits soar,
Creating joy forevermore.

Stars become our laughter's song,
Painting the world where we belong.
As twilight turns the day to dream,
Cheer sparkles, a radiant beam.

Sunlit Pathways to Wonder

Beneath the trees, the shadows dance,
Golden rays offer a chance.
Whispers of leaves in gentle sway,
Guide our hearts along the way.

Footsteps soft on a mossy floor,
Nature's beauty opens the door.
A hidden stream sings a sweet tune,
Inviting us to linger soon.

With every breath, the world awakes,
Every step, a new path makes.
Sunlit rays and laughter blend,
On this journey, we transcend.

Sparkles in the Everyday

A morning cup, steam rising high,
Sunshine sparkles in the sky.
Laughter shared with those we love,
Little joys wrapped like a glove.

In busy streets, a glance can glow,
Moments treasured gently flow.
A stranger's smile, a warming light,
Filling hearts, making things bright.

Tiny wonders, a child's gaze,
Chasing clouds on summer days.
In the mundane, magic we find,
Sparkling moments, pure and kind.

The Treasure of Tender Moments

Soft whispers shared in the night,
Holding hands, everything feels right.
Quiet laughter, eyes that gleam,
In these moments, we dare to dream.

With every hug, the world slips away,
Time stands still in love's embrace.
Gentle glances and knowing smiles,
In tender moments, we gather miles.

A shared sunset, colors blaze,
Memories wrapped in a warm haze.
These treasures, though they seem quite small,
Build the heart where love stands tall.

Navigating Joyful Journeys

Set your sails for the skies so clear,
Every wave brings dreams near.
With friends beside, we chart our course,
Through stormy seas, we'll find our force.

Laughter echoing on the breeze,
Moments cherished, heart at ease.
Paths unknown call us to roam,
In each step, we're never alone.

With every mile, new horizons greet,
In every heart, adventure beats.
Navigating joy, come what may,
Together, we pave our way.

Laughter's Gentle Caress

In the warm embrace of morning light,
Joy dances softly, taking flight.
Whispers of giggles fill the air,
Moments of bliss, beyond compare.

Each chuckle shared, a golden thread,
Binding our hearts, as laughter spreads.
In simple joys, we find our grace,
Together we bask in laughter's embrace.

The Magic of Tiny Wonders

In blades of grass, a world unfolds,
Tiny creatures, stories told.
A dewdrop's shimmer, a sparkling glance,
Nature's treasures, a childlike dance.

In every corner, magic lies,
Found in the sky, or butterflies.
With open hearts, we gaze and see,
The beauty of small things, wild and free.

Chasing Sunbeams

We run through fields, with arms out wide,
Chasing sunbeams, our hearts collide.
Golden rays that kiss our skin,
Moments cherished, laughter within.

The sky bursts forth, a canvas bright,
Each hue a memory, pure delight.
We twirl and spin, as shadows play,
In the warmth of the sun, we drift away.

Blossom of Unrestrained Glee

Petals unfurl in vibrant hues,
Every blossom whispers news.
In the garden of dreams come true,
Life's happiness, fresh as dew.

A child's laughter fills the air,
Joyful moments that we share.
In the bloom where magic thrives,
We find the spark that lights our lives.

Shadows of Blissful Memories

In the quiet of the night,
Dreams dance like gentle light.
Echoes of laughter reside,
In the corners where we hide.

Faded pictures, smiles remain,
Whispers soft, joy and pain.
Time may pass, yet still it stays,
In our hearts, those golden days.

Starlit skies recall our song,
Moments cherished, never wrong.
Shadows linger, warmth in glow,
In the depths of all we know.

Memories weave a tapestry,
Of our lives, entwined, so free.
In the dusk, the past we seek,
Shadows whisper, soft and sleek.

A Journey through Glistening Days

Sunrise paints the morning bright,
With every step, we chase the light.
Through meadows lush and rivers fair,
Adventure waits, a breath of air.

Footprints left on paths once tread,
Stories told of dreams we said.
In laughter shared, our spirits soar,
For every day brings something more.

Glimmers dance on waters clear,
In nature's arms, we lose our fear.
With every moment, new and bold,
Our journey's tale forever told.

Beneath the stars, we raise our voice,
A symphony, a vibrant choice.
Through glistening days, we find our way,
In the heart of life, we wish to stay.

Heartfelt Whispers of Cheer

In the gentle breeze, we hear,
Softly spoken words of cheer.
Beneath the branches, laughter rings,
Echoing what devotion brings.

Through the valleys, joy does flow,
In every heart, a sacred glow.
Hand in hand, we find our place,
With smiles that time cannot erase.

Warmth of kindness, freely shared,
Every moment, love declared.
In the whispers of the night,
Hope ignites, forever bright.

With each sunrise, we renew,
A pledge of cheer, so pure, so true.
In every story, joy will steer,
A symphony of heartfelt cheer.

The Eruption of Exuberance

With laughter loud and spirits high,
We embrace the day, let worries fly.
Colors burst, a vibrant show,
In every heart, excitement grows.

Dance beneath the golden sun,
With every heartbeat, we are one.
Joy explodes like fireworks bright,
Illuminating the starry night.

Each moment sings, a wild cheer,
In the thrill, we have no fear.
Life's a canvas, bold and grand,
We paint our dreams with open hands.

Let the world witness our delight,
In exuberance, we take flight.
With every laugh, our souls enhance,
In the rhythm of joy, we dance.

Dance of the Heart's Light

In the twilight, shadows creep,
Whispers of the night, so deep.
Stars awaken, twinkling bright,
Hearts entwined in gentle flight.

Echoes of a soft embrace,
Time slows down, a dreamlike space.
With each beat, a rhythm sways,
In this dance, our spirits blaze.

Moonlight casts a silver glow,
Underneath, the soft winds blow.
Together lost in melodies,
A harmony, sweet as the breeze.

Veils of silence, we can share,
Every moment, pure and rare.
Boundless joy, the night ignites,
In the dance of the heart's lights.

Serenade of Silent Laughter

Between the lines of whispered dreams,
Silent laughter softly gleams.
In the shadows, secrets hide,
Joyful whispers, hearts collide.

Moments wrapped in gentle grace,
Every smile a warm embrace.
Stars may fall, but spirits rise,
In the hush, our laughter flies.

The world may fade, but we will stay,
In this serenade, come what may.
Silent echoes fill the air,
In our hearts, we always share.

Through the silence, we connect,
Every laughter, pure, direct.
In this song, we find our way,
A serenade of joy, we play.

Unwritten Pages of Happiness

Blank pages waiting to be filled,
With dreams and hopes, our hearts distilled.
Colors dance upon the white,
Brush of joy, both soft and bright.

In the margins, happiness spills,
With each laugh, the spirit thrills.
Every moment, a tale unfolds,
Unwritten pages, stories told.

Time weaves threads of golden hue,
A tapestry of me and you.
In the distance, futures gaze,
On unwritten paths, we blaze.

Each heartbeat marks a line anew,
The ink of life, a vibrant view.
Together, let our pages flow,
In the book of happiness we know.

The Sparkling Hours

In the dawn, the world awakes,
Golden light, the canvas makes.
Every hour, a precious gem,
Shining bright, like diadem.

Moments dance in vibrant hues,
Each tick brings a pair of shoes.
Step into joy, glide through the day,
In the sparkling hours, we play.

Afternoon sings a sweet refrain,
Butterflies caught in summer's rain.
Laughter echoes, soft and clear,
Each sparkling hour, we hold dear.

As twilight falls, a magic glow,
Stars ignite, our spirits flow.
In the night, our dreams take flight,
Cherishing these sparkling hours, bright.

Embrace of the Morning Sun

Soft light spills on waking ground,
Whispers of the dawn surround.
Birds take flight in golden hue,
Nature sings the day anew.

Gentle warmth upon my face,
Filling hearts with soft embrace.
Shadows dance as dreams take flight,
Morning's grace ignites the light.

A world reborn with hope's sweet kiss,
Each moment cherish, none to miss.
Reflections bloom in every heart,
As daylight calls for a fresh start.

In this glow, my spirit soars,
Named by love, it gently roars.
Embrace the sun, let worries wane,
In morning's arms, all joys remain.

Echoes of Delight

Laughter dances on the breeze,
Sweetest sounds, a heart's reprise.
Joy ignites in silent night,
Echoes linger, pure delight.

Memories woven, voices blend,
In every note, a cherished friend.
Whispers of love in starry skies,
Life's symphony never dies.

Moments shared like petals fall,
In the silence, hear love's call.
Echoes of the past ignite,
In every heartbeat, pure delight.

Singing softly, hearts entwined,
In this melody, we're defined.
Let the echoes softly play,
Forever etched, our bright array.

Wind in the Willows of Wonder

Beneath the trees, a whisper flows,
Secrets shared where the river goes.
Leaves dance lightly, spirits free,
Nature's breath, pure harmony.

Gentle breezes stir the air,
Songs of joy, everywhere.
Crickets chirp a lullaby,
In the willows, dreams soar high.

Night unfolds with stars aglow,
Guiding hearts where they wish to go.
In the quiet, wonder sighs,
With every rustle, time flies.

Among the shadows, peace abides,
In the stillness, love confides.
Wind in willows, stories spun,
In nature's cradle, we are one.

Canvas of Colorful Moments

Brushed with hues of every kind,
Memories painted in the mind.
Moments splash across the page,
Life unfolds at every stage.

Vivid strokes of laughter bright,
Coloring shadows with pure light.
Each detail adds to life's grand scheme,
In this canvas, we all dream.

Tapestry woven with threads of time,
Creating rhythm,—nature's rhyme.
Sparks of joy in fleeting days,
Artistry in simple ways.

Hold the brush, let colors flow,
In every heartbeat, let love show.
Create a world where dreams reside,
In this canvas, we abide.

Mosaic of Merry Memories

In the garden of our youth,
Colors bright and wild,
Each moment a little truth,
In laughter lightly piled.

Under sunlit, sky-blue days,
We danced in golden light,
Every echo softly plays,
A canvas pure and bright.

Fragments of our sweetest times,
Captured in a frame,
Whispers of forgotten chimes,
Each memory a flame.

With every glance we share,
Heartbeats skip a beat,
In that mosaic we declare,
Life's moments are so sweet.

Euphony of Laughter

In the air, a giggle flows,
Like rivers full of cheer,
Mirroring the sun's warm glow,
It dances, light and clear.

Joyful echoes fill the space,
Each voice a vibrant chord,
Together we embrace the grace,
In laughter's sweet reward.

Beneath the starlit skies,
We weave our joyful song,
With every note that flies,
Our spirits dance along.

The symphony of glee we make,
A treasure ever true,
In every smile, a chance to wake,
The joy that lives in you.

Luminous Waves of Bliss

Upon the shore where dreams arise,
The ocean whispers low,
In silver hues beneath the skies,
The tides of love will flow.

As moonlight kisses gentle sands,
We drift in soft embrace,
Together crafting future plans,
In this enchanted place.

Every wave a heartbeat shared,
Every breeze a sigh,
In this moment, we are paired,
Beneath the endless sky.

With every rise and fall we feel,
The pulse of pure delight,
In each wave, a love that's real,
A dance of day and night.

Inspired by the Skylarks' Song

High above in skies of blue,
Skylarks sing their tune,
With melodies that feel brand new,
Their joy a sweet monsoon.

Every note, a gentle sway,
Carried on the breeze,
Inviting hearts to dance and play,
Beneath the rustling trees.

In vibrant fields where blossoms grow,
Their symphony takes flight,
A celebration of the glow,
Of nature's pure delight.

With every song, the world awakes,
Soft whispers of the dawn,
Inspired by what nature makes,
Together we move on.

The Art of Abundant Joy

In laughter's echo, hearts align,
Every moment, blissful shine.
With open arms, we let love flow,
In the art of joy, we find our glow.

Simple pleasures, a fleeting song,
In shared smiles, where we belong.
Painting life with vibrant hues,
In gratitude, we find our muse.

Dancing softly through every trial,
Finding blessings, mile by mile.
With each heartbeat, joy will rise,
Together beneath the vast skies.

Let's weave the threads of cheer and grace,
In this journey, find our place.
The art we craft in unity,
A masterpiece of harmony.

Ripple Effects of Glee

A laughter shared, a joyful sound,
In every heart, good vibes abound.
Throw kindness like a stone in stream,
Watch it ripple, build a dream.

In small acts, the joy ignites,
Lighting paths like twinkling lights.
From one soul to another's embrace,
Glee spreads forth, a warm grace.

Let smiles travel across the air,
Lift each other, show we care.
With every gesture, big or small,
The ripple of glee can touch us all.

Together we sing a joyful tune,
Beneath the sun, beneath the moon.
In unity, we raise our voice,
Creating hope, a wondrous choice.

Sunlit Paths of Positivity

Beneath the skies, so clear and bright,
We walk the paths of pure delight.
With every step, a dance we choose,
In the warmth of sun, we cannot lose.

Each sunrise, a chance to start anew,
In hues of gold, our dreams pursue.
In nature's arms, we find our peace,
From life's tension, we seek release.

With open hearts, we share the light,
Chasing shadows, banishing fright.
A positive spark in every soul,
Together, we can make life whole.

Through sunlit paths, we dare to roam,
With love as our guide, we find our home.
In laughter, hope, and dreams we trust,
With every step, it's love we must.

Embracing Lightness

In gentle whispers, kindness flows,
Like petals dancing in the prose.
Embracing lightness, hearts take flight,
In every smile, the world feels right.

We cast away our heavy chains,
Releasing burdens, breaking pains.
In simple joys, we find our way,
In the lightness, we choose to stay.

With laughter bright, we lift the veil,
Together we create a tale.
In moments fleeting, joy is found,
In lightness, our spirits are unbound.

Let's cherish the beauty of today,
With open hearts, come what may.
Embracing lightness, hand in hand,
In this journey, together we stand.

The Glow of Golden Moments

In the hush of twilight fades,
Golden rays with soft cascades.
Whispers call through fading light,
Memories spark, they take flight.

Each heartbeat shares a secret song,
Time stands still, it feels so strong.
With laughter wrapped in sunlit glow,
We cherish treasures, let them flow.

The clock may tick, the shadows play,
But golden moments won't decay.
They linger sweet in heart's embrace,
In every smile, their warm trace.

So hold them close, these radiant finds,
They weave the fabric of our minds.
A tapestry of love we weave,
In golden hues, we shall believe.

Fleeting Glimpses of Uplift

Like flashes of light in a dreary day,
Fleeting glimpses take the clouds away.
A gentle smile, a warm hello,
In simple moments, our spirits grow.

The laughter shared on a crowded street,
A kindred soul, a heart that beats.
In every gesture, joy ignites,
We chase the gray with pure delights.

Though temporal, they spark the bright,
Glimpses of hope, a guiding light.
So pause a while, let joy unfold,
In fleeting glimpses, life's beauty's told.

Let not the days slip past unseen,
Embrace the joy, the in-between.
For in each moment, we uplift,
Creating love, a precious gift.

When Souls Find Their Dance

In the rhythm of the night we sway,
Two hearts entwined, come what may.
Underneath the stars' romance,
A sacred space, when souls find dance.

With whispered secrets, our feet align,
Every movement tells a sign.
Lost in music, the world fades away,
Together we shine, come what may.

With each twirl, the magic spins,
A beautiful story where love begins.
Feel the warmth, the gentle trance,
In this moment, we find our chance.

With open hearts and spirits high,
We glow like constellations in the sky.
Together we dance, forever free,
When souls unite, it's harmony.

The Savor of Sweet Smiles

Sweet smiles shared in morning light,
A simple glance, a heart takes flight.
With every curve, warmth bestowed,
In each expression, joy overflowed.

The savor of laughter, like honeyed wine,
Moments sweet, forever entwined.
A melody sung through one's embrace,
In every smile, we find our place.

Each grin a treasure, a gift to hold,
A radiant story gently told.
Through trials faced and dreams we chase,
We share the love, the smiles we trace.

So let us cherish the sweet delight,
In warmth of kindness, shining bright.
For every smile is life's precious art,
A simple joy that fills the heart.

Flickers of Brightness

In shadows deep, a light will glow,
A spark of hope, a gentle show,
Through darkest nights, it finds its way,
A flicker bright, to guide the stray.

Embers dance in the silent air,
Whispers soft, a tender prayer,
Each moment counts, a chance to shine,
Flickers bright, the world divine.

In laughter shared, in kindness shown,
These tiny lights, they spark and sown,
Together they create a sea,
Of brightness pure, to set us free.

So cherish small, those bits of light,
They lead us through the longest night,
With every flicker, hope will rise,
A beacon bright beneath the skies.

Melodies of the Heart's Delight

In quiet moments, music sways,
A gentle tune that lifts our days,
Notes like petals fall and rise,
Melodies dance like butterflies.

With every chord, a story told,
Echoes warm, and spirits bold,
Heartbeats rhythm, soft and sweet,
In every sound, our lives complete.

Whispers soft as twilight dreams,
In harmony, our laughter gleams,
Each note a brushstroke on the soul,
Melodies weave us, make us whole.

So let the music fill the air,
With every breath, our joys we share,
In every heart, a symphony,
Of love and peace, our destiny.

The Art of Gratitude

In every day, a gift bestowed,
Moments small, a humble ode,
To recognize with open eyes,
The blessings vast beneath the skies.

A word of thanks, a smile shared,
With kindred hearts, we feel prepared,
To gather joy, both near and far,
In gratitude, our souls will spar.

For every trial, a lesson learned,
In grit and grace, our hearts have turned,
Each struggle brings a chance to see,
The art of gratitude sets us free.

So count each gift, both big and small,
In every step, we rise, we fall,
With grateful hearts, we bloom and grow,
In every moment, love will flow.

Pebbles of Positivity

Each little pebble on the shore,
A symbol of hope, forevermore,
Small and smooth, like whispered dreams,
Pebbles scattered, or so it seems.

Pick one up and hold it tight,
A token of joy, a spark of light,
In every grain, a story's found,
Pebbles of cheer, spread all around.

Toss them gently into the stream,
Watch the ripples, let your heart beam,
For every plop, a chance to see,
Positivity flows, wild and free.

So gather these gems, both bright and rare,
Let them remind you to always care,
In every step, let kindness steer,
With pebbles of joy, we conquer fear.

The Spark of Laughter

In the air, a giggle springs,
Light as feathers, joy that sings.
A dance of smiles across the room,
Chasing shadows, dispelling gloom.

Echoes bounce from wall to wall,
In this laughter, we stand tall.
Shared moments weave a golden thread,
Binding hearts, where fears have fled.

Tickling ribs and silly jest,
In this warmth, we feel our best.
Life's a stage, we play our part,
With every chuckle, we share our heart.

So let the spark ignite the night,
In laughter's glow, all feels right.
A simple gift, forever shared,
In joy's embrace, we are prepared.

Savoring Sunbeams

Golden rays on skin so warm,
Nature's touch, a gentle charm.
Dancing light through leafy trees,
Whispers carried on the breeze.

Each moment, a taste divine,
Sunlit dreams, a sweet design.
Colors burst, the world awakes,
In this warmth, my spirit breaks.

Crickets sing a serenade,
Under stars, a soft parade.
Delight in every shade and hue,
Finding peace in skies so blue.

With every breath, I breathe it in,
A sun-kissed life where joys begin.
Embracing light, the day anew,
In sunbeams' warmth, I feel so true.

Heartbeats of Happiness

In quiet moments, pulses rise,
Rhythms echo, life's sweet cries.
Every heartbeat, a song we play,
In this dance, we find our way.

Together we walk, side by side,
In the laughter, hearts collide.
Shared secrets, whispers in the night,
A tapestry of pure delight.

Through trials faced, we hold the line,
In every heartbeat, deep we shine.
Roots entwined, a strength we find,
In love's embrace, both bold and kind.

With each thump, joy we create,
In heartbeat's pulse, we celebrate.
Magical moments, forever new,
In every breath, I cherish you.

Glimmers of Gratefulness

In the quiet, reflections gleam,
Moments cherished, like a dream.
Soft whispers of the heart's delight,
In every glimmer, life feels bright.

Thankful for the paths we've walked,
In every word, our spirits talked.
Nature's gifts, both big and small,
With grateful eyes, I embrace them all.

The sun that rises, the moonlit glow,
In every season, love will flow.
Grateful for the bond we share,
In every heartbeat, in every prayer.

So let us count these treasures near,
In glimmers bright, we hold so dear.
With hearts alight, we'll sing our song,
In gratefulness, we all belong.

The Laughter that Lingers

In a room filled with cheer,
Joy dances around us.
Echoes of giggles persist,
A melody that we trust.

Memories wrapped in warmth,
Moments shared like a dream.
Laughter paints our hearts bright,
Together, we are a team.

Laughter is like sunshine,
Chasing shadows away.
With each chuckle and grin,
Hope blooms in our play.

Let it linger through time,
A treasure in our souls.
In the garden of friendship,
Laughter perfectly holds.

Unfurling Happiness

Like petals in the spring,
Happiness starts to spread.
Each moment a soft whisper,
Courage to forge ahead.

Beneath the azure sky,
Joy unfurls like a flag.
With every small victory,
No reason left to lag.

Through laughter and tears,
We rise and we grow.
Embracing all our flaws,
Together, we will glow.

As a flower in bloom,
Hearts open wide and free.
With love as our anchor,
We thrive in harmony.

Portraits of Positivity

Brushstrokes of bright colors,
On canvas, hope ignites.
Each smile a stroke of love,
Creating pure delights.

With every grateful heart,
We capture fleeting scenes.
In the gallery of life,
Positivity gleans.

Moments stitched with kindness,
Frame them, hold them near.
In the art of connection,
Our purpose becomes clear.

With laughter as our muse,
We paint a brighter world.
In portraits of positivity,
Endless joy unfurled.

In the Embrace of Lively Moments

A dance in the moonlight,
Spirits lifted high.
Every heartbeat a rhythm,
Underneath the sky.

With friends by our side,
We savor what's here.
In the embrace of moments,
We conquer every fear.

The spark in our laughter,
A glow that won't fade.
Chasing shadows away,
In memories we've made.

Together we capture,
All of life's sweet charms.
In the warmth of our laughter,
Forever safe in our arms.

A Breath of Delighted Air

In gentle whispers, breezes flow,
With every sigh, the blossoms glow.
Moments captured, sweet and rare,
We find our joy in a breath of air.

Soft sunlight dances on the ground,
Where colors mingle, joy is found.
Nature's gift, a soothing tune,
Inviting peace beneath the moon.

In laughter shared, hearts intertwine,
In every glance, pure love defines.
The world feels light, the spirit soars,
In this embrace, our happiness pours.

Glimmers of Blankets of Laughter

Beneath the stars, we share our dreams,
Wrapped in warmth, the laughter beams.
Stories flutter, like firelight,
In the quiet glow of a joyful night.

Echoes rise from souls so free,
Together, we blend in harmony.
Glimmers of hope in every voice,
We find in laughter, a world of choice.

The night unfolds with a gentle grace,
In each warm hug, we find our place.
A dance of joy, a spark ignites,
Glimmers of love in soft twilight.

The Color Palette of Contentment

Brush strokes wide, in hues so bright,
Each moment captured, pure delight.
The canvas whispers stories old,
Of dreams in colors, bold and gold.

With every shade that graces the heart,
Life's masterpiece, a work of art.
Moments blend, from dusk till dawn,
In painted joy, we carry on.

Textures mingle, soft and fair,
Threaded tightly, love fills the air.
In every corner, beauty flows,
The color palette, our spirits glow.

Essentials of Elation

A sip of joy in the morning light,
Hope hangs soft, a future bright.
With open arms, we greet the day,
In little things, our pains decay.

Laughter echoes in the hallway,
Each simple act, a reason to stay.
Connection blooms in every glance,
In shared delight, our hearts dance.

Through trials faced, our spirits rise,
In kindness shown, true beauty lies.
Essentials of elation, treasures rare,
In love's embrace, we find our share.

A Symphony of Simple Pleasures

In the morning light we greet,
The warmth of sun, the soft heart's beat.
Nature's whispers, gentle and clear,
A symphony played for all who hear.

With laughter shared and stories spun,
Every moment cherished, each one begun.
Footsteps dance on the fresh, green grass,
Life's playful tune, as moments pass.

The rustle of leaves, the call of birds,
A soothing balm without the words.
Each heartbeat syncs with nature's song,
In simple pleasures, we all belong.

The Brightness Beneath Our Feet

Through petals bright and vibrant hues,
A carpet laid of nature's muse.
With every step, a joy unfolds,
A world of wonder, bright and bold.

In garden paths where shadows play,
The light dances, guiding our way.
Each blade of grass, a story shared,
Beneath our feet, the earth revered.

From golden sun to silver moon,
The brightness shifts, like a sweet tune.
With every glance and every breath,
We find the joy in life, not death.

Sunshine in a Cup

A warm embrace in porcelain white,
Steam curling up, a sweet delight.
The taste of sunshine, bright and warm,
In every sip, we feel its charm.

Honey drips, a sweetness true,
With every sip, the heart renews.
A moment's pause in life's great race,
Sunshine captured in a warm embrace.

Chasing clouds away with glee,
In a simple cup, pure harmony.
So savor now, this nectar's bliss,
A cup of sunshine, can't resist.

Garden of Gleeful Thoughts

In the quiet corners, thoughts take flight,
Colors blooming, pure and bright.
Seeds of joy in soil are sown,
A garden nurtured, love has grown.

Whispers dance in the evening air,
Dreams unfurl with tender care.
Each flower speaks of hope anew,
In this garden, hearts break through.

With every petal, laughter rings,
A symphony of what joy brings.
In gleeful thoughts, we find our way,
As night turns soft to crown the day.

Radiating Warmth

In the glow of the setting sun,
Hearts embrace, and fears come undone.
A gentle touch, a soothing night,
In each smile, the world feels right.

Memories swirl like autumn leaves,
In the warmth of love, the spirit believes.
A cup of tea, a shared delight,
Together we chase the fading light.

Flickers of Fun

Laughter dances in the air,
Moments precious, moments rare.
Chasing dreams on a bright blue sky,
With friends around, we learn to fly.

Games and giggles fill the day,
In every corner, joy finds its way.
We twirl and spin, no time to waste,
In the heart of youth, life is embraced.

The Radiance of Today

Each sunrise brings a brand new start,
With colors bright to warm the heart.
The present glows, a splendid show,
In every moment, love will flow.

Let worries fade like morning mist,
Embrace the now, we can't resist.
With open arms, we seize the hour,
Together basking in life's power.

A Tapestry of Laughter

Threads of joy woven so tight,
In every chuckle, pure delight.
Stories shared across the room,
In laughter's glow, we find our bloom.

Kites soar high, under blue skies,
With every giggle, spirits rise.
A tapestry rich with tales untold,
In every heart, the warmth unfolds.

The Harmony of Heartbeats

In the stillness, whispers play,
A rhythm soft, night and day.
Each pulse a song, a dance so sweet,
In heart's embrace, our souls do meet.

Echoes linger, time stands still,
With every beat, we find our will.
A gentle hum, shared in the night,
Two hearts entwined, a perfect sight.

Through valleys deep, we walk as one,
In harmony, we greet the sun.
With every breath, the world takes pause,
In beat and bond, we find the cause.

Together we weave, a symphony,
In the dance of life, eternally.
With love's sweet sound, we float and soar,
Through rhythms bright, forevermore.

Festival of the Free Spirit

In laughter's glow, we come alive,
With spirits high, we learn to thrive.
Dancing under a starlit sky,
The world our stage, we learn to fly.

Colorful dreams, like petals flow,
In wild embrace, our hearts will grow.
Each moment captured, bright and bold,
A tapestry of tales retold.

Voices blend in joyous sound,
With every step, magic is found.
Unchained we run, through fields of gold,
In freedom's dance, our dreams unfold.

Together we spark, the night ignites,
In shadows cast, we chase the lights.
With open arms, the world we greet,
In the festival, love is our beat.

A Tapestry of Grins

In corners bright, a smile ignites,
A thread of joy in gentle sights.
With laughter shared, our spirits blend,
In every glance, we find a friend.

Mirthful whispers in the air,
We weave our dreams without a care.
Each grin a piece, a story spun,
In radiant hues, we come undone.

A joyful knot, our hearts entwine,
In every chuckle, love will shine.
Through trials faced, we hold on tight,
In every laugh, we find the light.

Together we craft, a vivid arc,
A canvas bright, where life leaves mark.
In this tapestry, we paint our fate,
In woven smiles, we celebrate.

Reflections in the Smile

A gentle curve, a spark on lips,
Holds stories deep, in fleeting sips.
Each smile a mirror, light does break,
In warmth displayed, our hearts awake.

From ups and downs, a tale unfolds,
In radiant hues, the warmth it holds.
Through every laugh, the world we see,
In sparkling eyes, we find the key.

The whispers soft, in glances shared,
A realm of hope, where dreams are bared.
In joy's embrace, we learn to stay,
Reflections dance, in bright array.

A bridge between, our souls align,
In simple joy, our hearts entwine.
Through every smile, a bond takes flight,
In love's embrace, we find our light.

Waves of Whimsy

In the tale of ocean's dance,
Laughter rides the rolling waves,
Colors swirl in playful trance,
Joyful hearts the moment saves.

Whispers of the salty breeze,
Tickles of the sunlit rays,
With every splash, the spirit frees,
In nature's arms, the heart sways.

Footprints left on golden sands,
Memories of summer's grace,
Each ripple writes with gentle hands,
Evoking smiles upon each face.

As the tide ebbs and flows anew,
We dance to life's sweet melody,
In waves of whimsy, dreams come true,
Embracing joy's simplicity.

Heartstrings of Serenity

In the quiet of the night,
Soft whispers fill the air,
Moonlight bathes the world in light,
Gentle moments, free of care.

Nature hums a soothing song,
Crickets chirp, the stars gleam bright,
With each breath, we feel we belong,
In calmness, love's pure light.

Hearts entwined like branches grow,
Rooted deep in trust's embrace,
In peaceful nights, our spirits glow,
Finding solace in each space.

Together in this sacred hush,
We weave our dreams, a tender thread,
In heartstrings, a gentle rush,
Where endless love is softly fed.

The Sweetness of Togetherness

In laughter's echo, voices blend,
Moments shared in warm embrace,
Hands held tight, our hearts transcend,
In unity, we find our place.

With every meal, stories unfold,
Flavors rich in every bite,
In love's warmth, our dreams are told,
Togetherness, a pure delight.

Through life's storms, we stand as one,
Facing trials, we won't break,
With kindness, brighter days will come,
In each other, our hearts awake.

The sweetness blooms in every glance,
A treasure trove of cherished days,
In every memory, love's dance,
Together, we'll always find our way.

Conversations with Contentment

In quiet corners, thoughts arise,
Gentle words weave through the air,
With open hearts and trusting eyes,
In stillness, we find solace there.

Sharing dreams beneath the trees,
Secrets whispered, soft and low,
In this moment, time does cease,
As wisdom's seeds begin to grow.

Laughter fills the spaces wide,
Each exchange, a thread of gold,
In kindness' glow, we confide,
Heartfelt stories gently told.

Together, we paint the sky,
With strokes of love and pure intent,
In conversations warm and spry,
We flourish in sweet content.

Whispers of Elation

Soft echoes drift on gentle breeze,
Lifting hearts like swaying trees.
In laughter's glow, we find our way,
A dance of light in the brightest day.

Moments cherished, like drops of rain,
Each sparkling tear, a joy, not pain.
Voices sing in harmony sweet,
Together we rise, in love's heartbeat.

With whispers sweet, our souls ignite,
Painting the dark with colors bright.
In twilight's kiss, our dreams take flight,
Together we weave, through day and night.

Hand in hand, we walk this trail,
With every breath, our spirits sail.
A tapestry woven, a story told,
In whispers of elation, our hearts unfold.

Radiant Echoes

In the morning light, we start anew,
With radiant echoes of me and you.
Through fields of gold, we wander wide,
Together as one, our hearts collide.

The sun kisses the earth with grace,
Each moment shared, a warm embrace.
In laughter's ring, we find our song,
A melody sweet, where we belong.

With every step, the shadows fade,
In vibrant hues, our joy displayed.
As life unfolds, like petals unfurled,
Radiant echoes light up the world.

In twilight's glow, let spirits soar,
Through whispered dreams, we search for more.
With every heartbeat, love grows bold,
In radiant echoes, our stories told.

Uplifted Spirits

As daylight breaks, our spirits rise,
Chasing the dawn, beneath bright skies.
With every step, the world anew,
Uplifted spirits, me and you.

In fleeting moments, we find our song,
Together we journey, where we belong.
Nature sings while the soft winds play,
Guiding our hearts, come what may.

With open arms, we greet the day,
Sharing laughter in our own way.
In every heartbeat, joy's refrain,
Uplifted spirits, free as the rain.

Gathered close, through thick and thin,
Together we dance, let the light in.
In the symphony of life, we're tuned,
Uplifted spirits, forever attuned.

A Dance of Delight

Under starlit skies, we twirl and sway,
In a dance of delight, night turns to day.
With whispered dreams and laughter's grace,
We find our joy in this sacred space.

Each movement bold, yet soft as air,
Together we weave, a love so rare.
In every twirl, our hearts sync in rhythm,
A beautiful sight, a shared prism.

As shadows fade, the dawn arrives,
In vibrant hues, our spirit thrives.
With open hearts, we chase the light,
In a dance of delight, everything feels right.

Let the world fade, just you and I,
In every heartbeat, our spirits fly.
In this endless waltz, with love as our guide,
A dance of delight, forever side by side.

Chronicles of Cheerfulness

In garden bright, the flowers bloom,
Butterflies dance, dispelling gloom.
Laughter echoes in the sun,
Joyful hearts, together, run.

With every dawn, a brand new start,
Grateful whispers fill each heart.
Chasing dreams on winding trails,
Carried forth by gentle gales.

The skies alight with vibrant hues,
Each moment brings a joyful muse.
With open arms and smiling eyes,
We lift our spirits to the skies.

In this tale of love and cheer,
Together we conquer every fear.
Hand in hand, we'll always be,
The chronicles of you and me.

Breaths of Brilliance

In twilight's glow, we seek the light,
Every breath a spark, burning bright.
Moments captured, pure and clear,
Brilliance found in those we hold dear.

Stars above ignite our dreams,
As silver moonlight softly gleams.
Together we soar, high and free,
Embracing what's meant to be.

Through whispers soft, our spirits sing,
The beauty each new day can bring.
With open hearts and ready minds,
A world of wonder we will find.

Breaths of life, in every stride,
With love and laughter as our guide.
In this journey, hand in hand,
Together, we will make our stand.

Whispers of Elation

The morning dew, a gentle kiss,
A silent promise, purest bliss.
In every smile that lights the way,
Whispers of elation softly sway.

Through woods of green, we wander far,
Chasing dreams beneath each star.
The rustling leaves, a joyful song,
In nature's arms, where we belong.

In laughter shared and stories told,
The warmth of friendship, worth more than gold.
Embrace the joy that life bestows,
A garden of moments, forever grows.

With every step, let spirits soar,
The heart rejoices, craving more.
In the whispers of the night so deep,
Elation's promise, forever to keep.

Radiance in Every Breath

A single breath, the world awakes,
Moments woven, love that never shakes.
In laughter's ring and kindness' glow,
Radiance formed wherever we go.

The sun that rises, warm and bright,
Fills our hearts with pure delight.
As shadows dance and worries cease,
In every breath, we find our peace.

With every heartbeat, stories unfold,
Tales of warmth and joys untold.
In every hug, a spark ignites,
Radiance shining through the nights.

In the whispers of the morning air,
We find connection, personal and rare.
Through the journey, hand in hand,
In every breath, we understand.

Traces of Happy Footsteps

In the morning light we stride,
Leaving footprints, side by side.
Laughter echoes in the air,
Joyful moments, none compare.

With every step, the world feels bright,
Chasing dreams in pure delight.
Through the valleys, over hills,
Guided by our heart's warm thrills.

Memories linger, sweet and true,
In fields of gold, me and you.
Paths once wandered, now a trace,
Every journey holds a grace.

So let's traverse this joyful way,
Finding magic in each day.
Together, hand in hand, we roam,
These happy footsteps lead us home.

The Radiant Rhythm of Life

Life dances gently, beats anew,
In vibrant colors, rich and true.
A symphony of hearts combined,
In every moment, love we find.

The stars above begin to twirl,
The moonlight dips, and dreams unfurl.
With every breath, a song's embrace,
In this grand rhythm, we find our place.

From sunrise's glow to sunset's sigh,
We move with grace, we learn to fly.
Nature whispers, life's sweet tune,
Harmonizing beneath the moon.

In this dance, our spirits lift,
Moments cherished, precious gift.
Together in this blissful sway,
We feel the pulse of each new day.

Cascades of Cheer

Laughter tumbles like a stream,
Sparkling bright, a joyful dream.
Each drop of joy, a story shared,
In cascades, love is declared.

Breezes play with thoughts so light,
Whispers of hope, hearts take flight.
Sunshine splashes in golden beams,
Filling life with vibrant themes.

Through gardens lush, in colors bold,
Every petal, a tale untold.
Nature sings, a vibrant choir,
As we bask in pure desire.

In this moment, let us be,
Eager for what joy can see.
Cascades of cheer, we will embrace,
Together, in life's warm grace.

Wings of Exuberance

Let our spirits soar and glide,
With open hearts, we take the ride.
In the sky of boundless dreams,
We chase the light, or so it seems.

Together we weave through the air,
Unfurling joy, free from despair.
With every gust, we feel alive,
In this dance, we learn to thrive.

Radiant colors paint the morn,
In vibrant hues, our souls reborn.
Chasing wonders, side by side,
With wings of cheer, we will abide.

Through clouds we drift, embracing flight,
In the embrace of purest light.
With wings of exuberance, we roam,
In this vast sky, we find our home.

Milton Keynes UK
Ingram Content Group UK Ltd.
UKHW020936041024
449263UK00011B/551

9 789916 882474